Grades
4–5

STEP-BY-STEP

Word Ladder Challenge

WORKBOOK

D1528961

By Michelle Gajda, Certified Reading Specialist

PETER PAUPER PRESS, INC.
Rye Brook, New York

PETER PAUPER PRESS

In 1928, at the age of twenty-two, Peter Beilenson began printing books on a small press in the basement of his parents' home in Larchmont, New York. Peter—and later, his wife, Edna—sought to create fine books that sold at "prices even a pauper could afford."

Today, still family owned and operated, Peter Pauper Press continues to honor our founders' legacy of quality, value, and fun for big kids and small kids alike.

About the Author

Michelle Gajda is an elementary school teacher, reading specialist, adjunct professor, and recipient of a Massachusetts Reading Association Sylvia D. Brown Scholarship for action research in the field of literacy.

Designed by Heather Zschock

Copyright © 2023 Peter Pauper Press, Inc.
Manufactured for Peter Pauper Press, Inc.
3 International Drive
Rye Brook, NY 10573 USA

Published in the United Kingdom and Europe by
Peter Pauper Press, Inc. c/o White Pebble International
Units 2-3, Spring Business Park
Stanbridge Road
Havant, Hampshire PO9 2GJ, UK

ISBN 978-1-4413-4011-5
Printed in China

7 6 5 4 3 2 1

Dear Families, Guardians, and Educators,

What are word ladders? Word ladders are quick, fun activities that offer children the opportunity to play with words and language while building important foundational reading skills. Word ladders help children learn to manipulate letters and sounds, build vocabulary, and recognize spelling, pronunciation, and patterns in common phonograms. (A phonogram is a symbol, letter, or combination of letters that represent a sound. For example, /**igh**/ in the words **sigh** and **high**. Or /**ee**/ in the words **sheep** and **jeep**.)

Depending on their age and skill sets, children can complete word ladders independently by reading the clues provided on each rung of the ladder and filling in the appropriate words. Alternatively, an adult can serve as the reader and scribe for pre-readers and pre-writers.

How the Word Ladders Are Ordered

Children learn phonetic skills in a particular sequence (easier to more complex), and each skill builds on the ones taught and learned previously. The word ladders in this series of books were ordered (as much as possible) in the same sequence in which children learn them when learning to read. The beginning ladders in each of the series spiral back briefly to previously learned skills to ensure that children have mastered them (and to help build their confidence), before moving on to more complex phonics.

Ladders 1–13: **Vowel-Consonant-E Syllables with Beginning and Ending Blends**

Ladders 14–27: **Vowel Teams**

Ladders 28–48: **Advanced Digraphs/Trigraphs and Mixed Phonics**

Ladders 49–53: **R Controlled Vowels**

Ladders 54–56: **Mixed Phonics**

Ladders 57–60: **Consonant -le Syllable**

How to Use the Clues

Each rung will have two clues to help the reader figure out what the next word is. The first clue will either be a definition or description of the word, or a fill-in-the-blank sentence. The second clue will provide the reader with hints about whether they should replace, remove, or add a letter (or letters) using some basic phonics terminology:

- **vowels:** the letters A, E, I, O, U, and sometimes Y

- **consonants:** any letters other than vowels

- **blend:** when two letters come together and retain both of their sounds, such as *bl* in *blend*.
  examples: *bl, br, cl, cr, fl, fr, gl, gr, ld, mp, nt, pl, pt, sl, sm, sn, sp, st, sw, tr*

- **3-letter blend:** when three letters come together and retain their own sounds, such as *spr* in *sprint*.
  examples: *scr, spl, spr, str*

- **digraph:** when two letters come together resulting in one sound, such as *sh* in *sheep*.
  examples: *ch, ck, ea, gh, gn, kn, oe, ph, qu, sh, th, ue, wh*

- **consonant digraph blend:** a digraph with an additional voiced consonant, such as *shr* in *shrink*.
  examples: *nch, shr, squ, thr*

- **trigraph:** when three letters come together resulting in one sound, such as *igh* in *high*.
  examples: *awe, eau, eou, igh, iou*

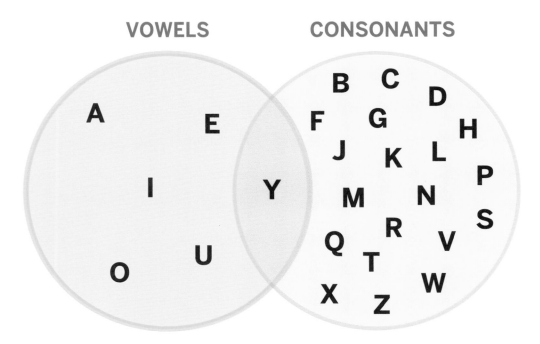

How Do Word Ladders Work?

- Start with the word on the bottom rung of each ladder.

- Read the clue on the next rung going up the ladder.

- You may be adding, deleting, or changing one to two letters on each rung. Use the clues and number of spaces provided on the rung to help determine the new word.

- Write the new word on the rung.

- Continue working your way up the ladder in the same manner for each rung until you reach the top.

Riddle Fun

On every fifth ladder page, there is a riddle to solve using letters found throughout the five previous word ladders. To find the answer to the riddle, match the numbered letters from the ladders to the corresponding numbers on the answer line.

Word ladders are a wonderful way for emerging readers to build their phonological awareness and sound-symbol relationship skills by adding, deleting, and changing sounds within simple words. Older children increase their vocabulary as they read and analyze the clues for each new word—strengthening their understanding of the words and word-related concepts such as definitions, parts of speech, word features (i.e. opposites, comparatives/superlatives, etc.). As you can see, word ladders provide many literacy learning opportunities in fun, short, digestable bits of time. And if you get stuck, there's an answer key in the back!

Have fun and happy climbing!

A fruit that grows in bunches
Change a consonant.

— — — — —

To rub or press into smaller pieces
Change the beginning consonant.

— — — — —

A box made of wood
Add a consonant.

— — — — —
4

The speed of something
Change the beginning consonant.

— — — —

A partner or friend
Change a vowel.

— — — —

To not speak
Change the beginning consonant.

— — — —

A rough string or twine
Change the beginning consonant.

— — — —

The opposite of ugly
Change the beginning consonant.

— — — —
1

A stringed instrument
Remove a consonant.

— — — —

NAME: _____

Start at the bottom and climb your way up by
reading the clues to change the word in each step.

FLUTE

Costume; dis_____
Change the beginning consonant and add a vowel.

— — — — — —

Knowledgeable
Change the beginning consonant.

— — — —

Sun_____, sunset
Change the vowel.

— — — —

A type of flower
Change the beginning consonant.

— — — —

To stand in the same position
over time, as a model
Change the beginning consonant.

— — — —
2

A part of your face
Change the beginning consonant.

— — — —

A long tube that water runs through
Remove a consonant.

— — — —

The opposite of these
Change the beginning digraph.

— — — — —

To have made a choice
Change the beginning blend to a digraph.

— — — —

NAME: _____

Start at the bottom and climb your way up by
reading the clues to change the word in each step.

CLOSE

The past tense of wear
Change a vowel.

→ _ _ _ _

Thin cording used to carry an electrical charge
Change a consonant.

→ _ _ _ _

The opposite of narrow
Change a vowel.

→ _ _ _ _

To walk in shallow water
Remove the beginning consonant and change the second consonant.

→ _ _ _ _

A sharp metal edge for cutting or shaving
Change the beginning blend to a different blend.

→ _ _ _ _
       3

An open space in a forest
Change the beginning blend to a different blend.

→ _ _ _ _ _
    5

The score you receive on a test or quiz
Change the beginning blend to a different blend.

→ _ _ _ _ _

To give one thing for another
Change the beginning blend to a different blend.

→ _ _ _ _ _

A tool used to dig in a garden
Change the beginning digraph to a blend.

→ _ _ _ _ _

NAME: _____

Start at the bottom and climb your way up by reading the clues to change the word in each step.

SHADE

The opposite of tall
Change the beginning blend to a digraph.

→ _ _ _ _ _

A loud noise from your nose
Change the beginning blend to a different blend.

→ _ _ _ _ _

A game played by a team
Add a consonant.

→ _ _ _ _

A body of water where a ship may dock
Change the beginning consonant.

→ _ _ _ _

To organize into categories
Change the final letter.

→ _ _ _ _

An ache or wound
Change a vowel.

→ _ _ _ _

To be positive/confident
Change the beginning consonant.

→ _ _ _ _

To attract
Change the beginning consonant.

→ _ _ _ _

Clean and not soiled
Change the beginning consonant.

→ _ _ _ _

NAME: _____

Start at the bottom and climb your way up by
reading the clues to change the word in each step.

CURE

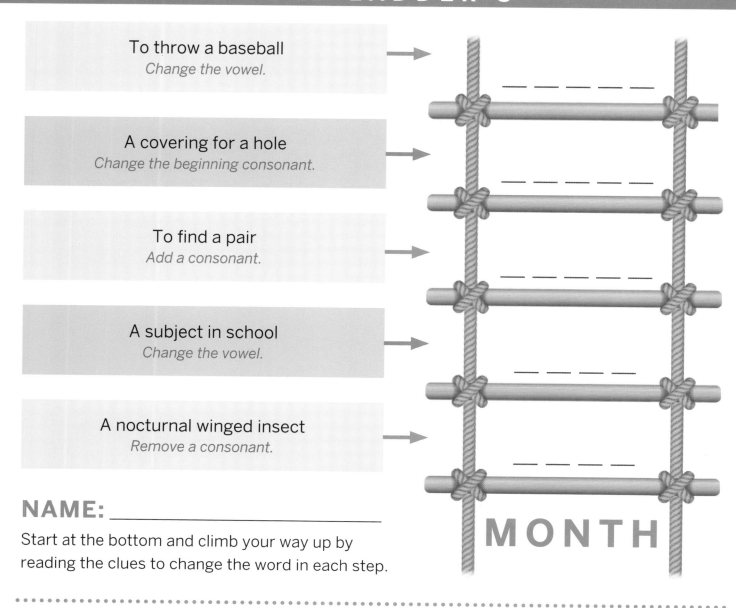

To throw a baseball
Change the vowel.

A covering for a hole
Change the beginning consonant.

To find a pair
Add a consonant.

A subject in school
Change the vowel.

A nocturnal winged insect
Remove a consonant.

MONTH

NAME: _____

Start at the bottom and climb your way up by
reading the clues to change the word in each step.

After you've completed the five prior word ladders, complete the riddle below by matching
the numbered letters from the ladders to the corresponding numbers on the answer line.

RIDDLE #1

**What has hands and a face but cannot
hold anything or smile?**

____ ____ ____ ____ ____ **K**
3   4   5   2   1

A type of fish
Remove a consonant.

_ _ _ _ _

A sharp metal peg
Change a vowel.

_ _ _ _

Past tense of speak
Change the beginning blend.

_ _ _ _ _

To add coal or fuel
Change a vowel.

_ _ _ _

A peg used to hold a tent in place
Change the beginning blend.

_ _ _ _

A reptile
Change the beginning digraph to a blend.

_ _ _ _
2

To pump up and down
Change the beginning blend to a digraph.

_ _ _ _ _

A small piece of something, like snow
Add a consonant.

_ _ _ _ _

A fresh body of water
Change a vowel.

_ _ _ _

NAME: _____

LIKE

Start at the bottom and climb your way up by
reading the clues to change the word in each step.

Checkers or chess
Change the beginning consonant.

_ _ _ _ _

To civilize
Change a vowel.

_ _ _ _ _
3

A large, heavy book
Change a vowel.

_ _ _ _ _

Hours, minutes, and seconds
Change the beginning consonant.

_ _ _ _ _

A fruit often paired with lemons
Change a vowel.

_ _ _ _ _

Uninspiring and dull
Remove a consonant.

_ _ _ _

A burst of fire
Change the beginning blend to a different blend.

_ _ _ _ _

To assign responsibility for a fault or wrong
Change the beginning blend to a different blend.

_ _ _ _ _

A solid border to put around a photo or picture
Add a consonant.

_ _ _ _ _
1

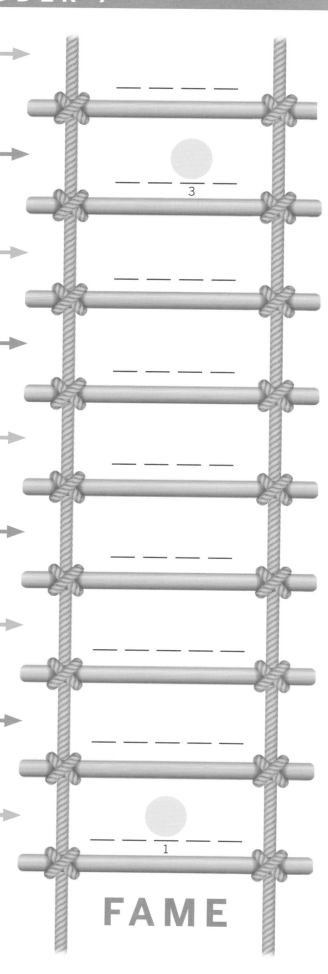

NAME: _____

Start at the bottom and climb your way up by
reading the clues to change the word in each step.

FAME

To have made a choice
Change the beginning blend to a digraph.

_ _ _ _ _ _

The opposite of open
Change the beginning blend to a different blend.

_ _ _ _ _

A style of writing
Add a consonant to make a beginning blend.

_ _ _ _ _

A type of flower
Change one consonant.

_ _ _ _

To follow a pattern by heart; repetition
Change both consonants.

_ _ _ _ _
4

A small sheltered bay
Remove the blend and add a single consonant.

_ _ _ _

A group of trees that are the same type
Change a vowel.

_ _ _ _ _

A place to bury the dead
Change the beginning blend to a different blend.

_ _ _ _ _

A strong desire to do or have something
Change the beginning blend to a different blend.

_ _ _ _ _

NAME: _____

Start at the bottom and climb your way up by
reading the clues to change the word in each step.

BRAVE

WORD LADDER 9

An instrument used to measure/track time
Add a beginning consonant to create a blend.

_ _ _ _ _

A mechanism used to keep something secure that must be opened with a key
Change the beginning consonant.

_ _ _ _

The clock says "tick-____"
Remove a consonant.

_ _ _ _

The goods and merchandise in a store
Change a vowel.

_ _ _ _

A piece of wood from a tree or bush
Change the beginning blend to a different blend.

_ _ _ _

Slippery and wet
Change the final vowel.

_ _ _ _

A cut piece of something (such as pie)
Change the beginning consonant to a blend.

_ _ _ _

A bug that nests in human hair and scalp
Change the beginning consonant.

_ _ _ _

6-sided cubes with dots
Change the beginning consonant.

_ _ _ _

NAME: _____

Start at the bottom and climb your way up by reading the clues to change the word in each step.

MICE

WORD LADDER 10

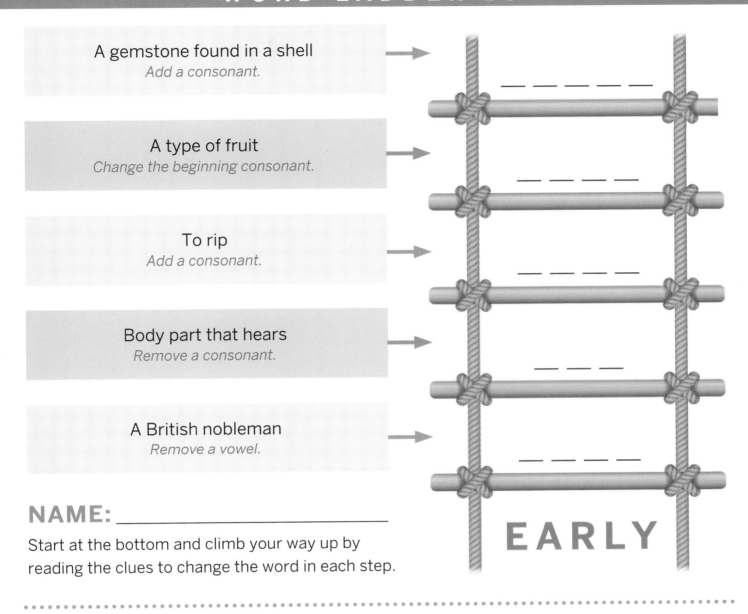

A gemstone found in a shell
Add a consonant.

A type of fruit
Change the beginning consonant.

To rip
Add a consonant.

Body part that hears
Remove a consonant.

A British nobleman
Remove a vowel.

EARLY

NAME: _____

Start at the bottom and climb your way up by
reading the clues to change the word in each step.

After you've completed the five prior word ladders, complete the riddle below by matching
the numbered letters from the ladders to the corresponding numbers on the answer line.

RIDDLE #2

It belongs to you, but your friends use it more.
What is it?

YOUR ____ ____ ____ ____
             2   1   3   4

A place to put religious items to worship
Add a consonant.

— — — — ◯ — — —
1

To be in the light/to glow
Change the beginning digraph to a different digraph.

— — — — —

To talk in a shrill, pouty voice
Add a consonant.

— — — —

An alcoholic beverage made from grapes
Change the beginning consonant.

— — — —

A type of evergreen tree
Change the beginning consonant.

◯ — — —
2

A type of winding plant
Change a vowel.

— — — —

A thin object that rotates, often used to indicate the wind's direction.
Change the beginning consonant.

— — — —

A small road or path
Remove a consonant.

— — — —

A vehicle that travels in the sky
Add a vowel.

— — — —

NAME: _____

Start at the bottom and climb your way up by reading the clues to change the word in each step.

PLAN

A long, strong step
Change a consonant and add a consonant.

_____ remark; derogatory or mocking
Change the beginning blend to a different blend.

Playground fixture
Change the beginning blend to a different blend.

To move smoothly
Change the beginning digraph to a blend.

To blame in a teasing way
Change the beginning blend to a digraph.

A partner in a wedding party
Change the beginning consonant to a blend.

You can play in___ or out____.
Change the beginning consonant.

The flow of the ocean's water
Change the beginning consonant.

The opposite of narrow
Change the beginning consonant.

NAME: _____

HIDE

Start at the bottom and climb your way up by
reading the clues to change the word in each step.

To become unfrozen
Change the beginning digraph.

_ _ _ _

Nibble, as on a bone
Change the beginning blend to a digraph.

_ _ _ _

To make marks on paper or other surfaces
Remove a consonant.

_ _ _ _

The past tense of draw
Change the beginning consonant to a blend.

_ _ _ _ _

Involuntary mouth motion when bored or tired
Change the beginning consonant.

_ _ _ _
4

Area of grass
Add a consonant.

_ _ _ _

A rule that is enforced
Remove a consonant.

_ _ _ _

An imperfection or mark in something
Change the beginning blend to a different blend.

_ _ _ _

The sharp part of an animal's paw or foot
Add a consonant to create a blend.

_ _ _ _

NAME: _____

CAW

Start at the bottom and climb your way up by
reading the clues to change the word in each step.

To gather or collect
Change the final consonant.

⬤ 5 _ _ _ _

To decode print on a page
Remove a digraph and add a single consonant.

_ _ _ _

To extend an arm out
Remove a consonant.

_ _ _ _ _

To talk about your ideas and values
Add a consonant to create a beginning blend.

_ _ _ _ _ _

A type of fruit with a fuzzy outer skin
Change the beginning consonant.

_ _ _ _ _

To instruct
Change the beginning consonant.

_ _ _ _ _

To drain something away (usually from soil)
Remove a consonant.

_ _ _ _ _

A chemical used for cleaning
Change the beginning blend to a different blend.

_ _ _ _ _ _

Breaking or failing to observe a law
or agreement
Add a consonant.

_ _ _ _ _ _ _

NAME: _____

Start at the bottom and climb your way up by
reading the clues to change the word in each step.

BEACH

WORD LADDER 15

Conflict
Add a consonant to create a blend.

— — — — —

Money
Change the blend to a digraph.

— — — —

A covering put on a broken bone
Change the vowel.

— — — —

The value of something to purchase
Change the beginning consonant.

— — — —
⁷

The opposite of found
Change the beginning blend to a single consonant.

— — — —
⁶

NAME: _____

Start at the bottom and climb your way up by
reading the clues to change the word in each step.

FROST

After you've completed the five prior word ladders, complete the riddle below by matching
the numbered letters from the ladders to the corresponding numbers on the answer line.

RIDDLE #3

If you don't keep me, I'll break. What am I?

___ ___ ___ ___ **M** ___ ___ ___
4   2   5   6   1   7   3

To guide the movement of
(such as a car or truck)
Change the beginning consonant to a blend.

_ _ _ _ _

A forest animal
Change the final consonant.

_ _ _ _

The opposite of shallow
Change the beginning consonant.

_ _ _ _

To save
Change the beginning consonant.

_ _ _ _

To cry
Change the beginning consonant.

_ _ _ _

To spread out and soak into
Remove a consonant.

_ _ _ _

An animal that produces wool
Change the beginning blend to a digraph.

1 _ _ _ _

To close your eyes and rest your body
Change the beginning blend to a different blend.

_ _ _ _ _

A sharp incline, as a flight of stairs
Change the beginning blend to a different blend.

_ _ _ _ _

NAME: _____

Start at the bottom and climb your way up by
reading the clues to change the word in each step.

SWEEP

Food or items used to catch something
Change the beginning consonant.

→ _ _ _ _
2

A style of walking or moving
Remove the beginning blend and add a single consonant.

→ _ _ _ _

A narrow passage of water that connects two larger bodies of water
Add a consonant.

→ _ _ _ _ _ _

A feature that identifies someone
Change the beginning blend to a different blend and change the final consonant.

→ _ _ _ _ _

The opposite of fancy
Change the beginning blend to a different blend.

→ _ _ _ _ _

To have killed
Change the beginning blend to a different blend.

→ _ _ _ _ _

A mark or imperfection of color on something
Remove a consonant.

→ _ _ _ _

To pull or push to a breaking point
Add a consonant.

→ _ _ _ _ _

Transportation on rails
Add a consonant.

→ _ _ _ _

NAME: _____

Start at the bottom and climb your way up by reading the clues to change the word in each step.

RAIN

Water around a castle
Change the beginning blend to a single consonant.

⟶ ◯
3 _ _ _ _

To be buoyed on water
Change the beginning blend to a different blend.

⟶ _ _ _ _ _

To brag
Change the beginning consonant to a blend.

⟶ _ _ _ _

A farm animal
Change the beginning consonant.

⟶ _ _ _

A winter clothing garment
Change the final consonant.

⟶ _ _ _ _

A black lumpy fuel source
Change the beginning consonant.

⟶ _ _ _ _

A mission to accomplish
Change the final consonant.

⟶ _ _ _ _

Provoke or annoy someone
Change the beginning consonant.

⟶ _ _ _ _

A path that cars drive on
Change the beginning consonant.

⟶ _ _ _ _

NAME: _____

TOAD

Start at the bottom and climb your way up by
reading the clues to change the word in each step.

60 minutes
Change the beginning consonant.

— — — —

The opposite of sweet
Remove a consonant.

— — — —

To scrub hard
Change the final consonant.

— — — —

Eagle ____, boy ____ or girl ____
Change the beginning digraph to a blend.

— — — —

To yell
Change the beginning blend to a digraph.

— — — —

A pig's nose
Change the beginning blend to a different blend.

— — — —

Part of a fountain where water comes out of
Remove a consonant.

— — — —
4

The early beginning of a plant
Change the beginning blend to a 3-letter blend.

— — — —

Somewhat fat or heavy
Change the beginning blend to a different blend.

— — — —

NAME: _____

Start at the bottom and climb your way up by
reading the clues to change the word in each step.

TROUT

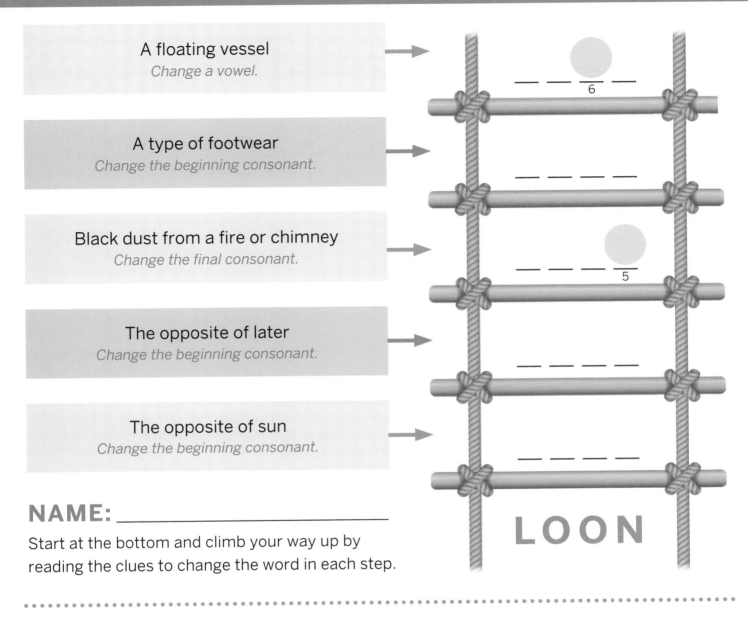

A floating vessel
Change a vowel.

___ ___ ___ ___
            6

A type of footwear
Change the beginning consonant.

___ ___ ___ ___

Black dust from a fire or chimney
Change the final consonant.

___ ___ ___ ___
            5

The opposite of later
Change the beginning consonant.

___ ___ ___ ___

The opposite of sun
Change the beginning consonant.

___ ___ ___ ___

LOON

NAME: _____

Start at the bottom and climb your way up by
reading the clues to change the word in each step.

After you've completed the five prior word ladders, complete the riddle below by matching
the numbered letters from the ladders to the corresponding numbers on the answer line.

RIDDLE #4

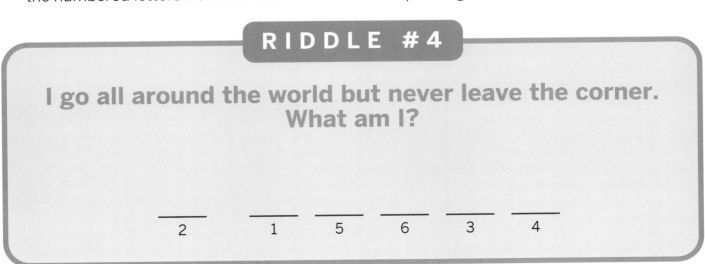

I go all around the world but never leave the corner.
What am I?

___ ___ ___ ___ ___ ___
 2   1   5   6   3   4

Our class ____ is on the third floor.
Change the beginning consonant.

→ _ _ _ _

Hannah will weave a scarf on the wooden ____.
Remove a consonant.

→ _ _ _ _

In the spring the flowers ____.
Change the beginning blend to a different blend.

→ _ _ _ _ _
                    1

Go sweep the porch with a ____.
Change the final consonant.

→ _ _ _ _ _

We played in the babbling ____ all day.
Change the beginning digraph to a blend.

→ _ _ _ _ _

The earthquake ____ the town.
Add a consonant.

→ _ _ _ _ _

Harper caught a fish on the ____ of her fishing rod.
Change the final consonant.

→ _ _ _ _

My sweatshirt has a ____.
Change the beginning consonant.

→ _ _ _

We stacked 3 piles of ____ near the fireplace.
Change the beginning consonant.

→ _ _ _ _

NAME: _____

Start at the bottom and climb your way up by reading the clues to change the word in each step.

GOOD

The athlete pulled their _____ muscle jumping over the hurdle.
Change the beginning consonant to a blend.

⟶ _ _ _ _ _

I hope you will _____ the team.
Change the beginning consonant.

⟶ _ _ _ _

I have a silver _____ in my wallet.
Change the final consonant.

⟶ _ _₂ _

The snake will _____ in the round basket.
Change the beginning blend to a single consonant.

⟶ _₆ _ _ _

The milk will _____ if you leave it out too long.
Change the beginning blend to a different blend.

⟶ _ _ _ _ _

My dad will _____ the scallops in the oven.
Add a consonant to create a blend.

⟶ _ _ _ _ _

Wait for the water to _____ before you add the pasta.
Change the beginning consonant.

⟶ _ _ _ _

Mike had to _____ in the hot sun to get his work done.
Change the beginning consonant.

⟶ _ _ _ _

Cover the pie with _____ before you bake it.
Change the beginning consonant.

⟶ _ _ _ _

NAME: _____

SOIL

Start at the bottom and climb your way up by reading the clues to change the word in each step.

WORD LADDER 23

Water pollution is a _____ to sea animals.
Change the final consonant.

_ _ _ _ _ _

I use my needle and _____ to sew.
Add a consonant.

_ _ _ _ _

The _____ on my bike tire is wearing down.
Change the beginning blend to a different blend.

_ _ _ _ _

Giving an oral report fills me with _____.
Change the beginning blend to a different blend.

_ _ _ _ _

I like to eat whole wheat _____.
Change the beginning consonant to a blend.

_ _ _ _ _

I _____ my book until midnight.
Change the beginning consonant.

_ _ _ _

The pencil _____ is getting dull.
Change the beginning consonant.

_ _ _ _

_____, shoulders, knees, and toes
Change the beginning consonant.

_ _ _ _

Opposite of alive
Remove the 3-letter blend and replace with a single consonant.

_ _ _ _

NAME: _____

Start at the bottom and climb your way up by
reading the clues to change the word in each step.

SPREAD

Emma rode on the merry-go- _____ at the carnival.
Remove the final consonant and add two.

— — — — —
5

The troops retreat turned into a _____.
Remove two consonants.

— — — —

Our seeds will _____ in a few more days.
Add a consonant.

— — — — —

The water came streaming out of the _____.
Change the beginning blend to a different blend.

— — — —
4

The _____ man enjoyed a good, large meal.
Change the beginning blend to a different blend.

— — — —

Dave caught a rainbow _____ in the river.
Change one consonant.

— — — —

The carpenter will _____ the tiles in the bathroom.
Remove two consonants and add one.

— — — —

The _____ was slippery after it snowed.
Change the beginning consonant to a blend.

— — — —

I was _____ and determined to finish my report early.
Change the beginning consonant.

— — — — —

NAME: _____

POUND

Start at the bottom and climb your way up by reading the clues to change the word in each step.

Walt let out a loud ___ after he drank his soda.
Change the final consonant.

— — — —
　　　3

Be careful not to ____ yourself on the stove.
Change the vowel.

— — — —

What year were you ____?
Change the beginning consonant.

— — — —

The map was ____ into two pieces.
Remove a consonant.

— — — —

I pricked my finger on a _____ on the rosebush.
Add a consonant.

— — — — —
　　　　7

NAME: _____

Start at the bottom and climb your way up by reading the clues to change the word in each step.

HORN

After you've completed the five prior word ladders, complete the riddle below by matching the numbered letters from the ladders to the corresponding numbers on the answer line.

RIDDLE #5

I make a loud sound when I am changing. When I do change, I get bigger but weigh less. What am I?

___ ___ ___ ___ ___ ___ ___
3　1　4　6　2　5　7

The dog will _____ to the corner when his owner yells.
Change the beginning blend to a different blend.

— — — — —

The garbage is beginning to _____.
Change the vowel.

— — — — —
        4

The rotten egg _____ up the entire kitchen.
Change the beginning blend to a different blend.

— — — —

We found treasure stored in the old _____ in the attic.
Change the beginning blend to a different blend.

— — — —

The old woman had a lot of _____ and energy.
Change the beginning blend to a different blend.

— — — —

Rob was worried he was going to _____ out of school.
Change the final consonant.

— — — —

The road crew _____ the debris into the back of the truck.
Change the beginning blend to a different blend.

— — — —

The hiker _____ to the side of the cliff.
Add a consonant.

— — — — —
              1

Her right _____ was full of fluid.
Change the beginning consonant.

— — — — —

NAME: _____

Start at the bottom and climb your way up by reading the clues to change the word in each step.

HUNG

We ____ tomatoes, corn, and beans in our garden.
Change the beginning blend to a different blend.

— — — —

The artist ____ a picture of the landscape.
Change the beginning blend to a different blend.

— — — —

Ship's mates
Change the vowel.

— — — —

Large black bird
Change the beginning blend to a different blend.

— — — —

The ____ of the ship got hit by a torpedo.
Remove a consonant.

— — — —

The jaguar will ____ through the jungle at night
Change the beginning blend to a different blend.

— — — —

She stomped into the room with a ____ on her face.
Change the beginning blend to a different blend.

— — — — —

The dog will ____ if you get too close.
Change the beginning consonant to a blend.

— — — — —
                    2

The wolf will ____ at the moon.
Change the beginning consonant.

— — — —

NAME: _____

Start at the bottom and climb your way up by reading the clues to change the word in each step.

FOWL

Jen learned a new ___ in sewing class.
Change the beginning blend to a different blend.

_ _ _ _ _

We had to ____ the kind of toothpaste we use.
Change the beginning consonant to create a blend.

_ _ _ _ _

A ____ might scare you on Halloween.
Change the beginning consonant.

_ _ _ _

The car got stuck in the _____.
Change the beginning consonant.

_ _ _ _

The batter swung at a wild _____.
Change the vowel.

_ _ _ _

Peter Rabbit snuck into the carrot _____.
Change the beginning consonant.

_ _ _ _

The ____ on the garden gate is broken.
Change the beginning consonant.

_ _ _ _ _

Light the ____ and start the fire.
Change the beginning consonant.

_ _ _ _ _
3

The baby chicks are about
to ____ from their eggs!
Change the beginning consonant.

_ _ _ _ _

NAME: _____

Start at the bottom and climb your way up by
reading the clues to change the word in each step.

WATCH

We ___ back and forth to get wood
for the fireplace all winter.
Change the beginning blend to a different blend.

→ _ _ _ _ _ _

The baby had a ____ of food
on his face after he ate.
Change the beginning blend to a different blend.

→ _ _ _ _ _

The company had to clean the _____ from
the river after the chemical spill.
Change the beginning blend to a different blend.

→ _ _ _ _ _

Lisa held a _____ against her friend
after they argued.
Change the beginning blend to a different blend.

→ _ _ _ _ _

It was such a ____ doing all of the
hard and boring work.
Change the beginning consonant to a blend.

→ _ _ _ _

My father gave me a ____ with his elbow.
Change the beginning consonant.

→ _ _ _ _

The criminal went before the ____ to
hear his punishment.
Change the beginning consonant.

→ _ _ _ _

I love to eat peanut butter
and chocolate _____.
Change the beginning consonant.

→ _ _ _ _

The dog would not ____ from the couch
when I wanted to sit down.
Change a vowel.

→ _ _ _ _

NAME: _____

Start at the bottom and climb your way up by
reading the clues to change the word in each step.

BADGE

I found a heart-shaped ____ on the dirt road.
Add a consonant.

My father's ____ let me know he was angry.
Change a vowel.

The musician played a lively ____ on his saxophone.
Change the beginning consonant.

____ is the first month of summer.
Change the beginning blend to a single consonant.

A ____ is a dried plum.
Change a vowel.

NAME: _____

Start at the bottom and climb your way up by reading the clues to change the word in each step.

5

PRONE

After you've completed the five prior word ladders, complete the riddle below by matching the numbered letters from the ladders to the corresponding numbers on the answer line.

RIDDLE #6

I can fill a room but take up no space. What am I?

____ ____ ____ ____ ____
 2   4   1   3   5

To swirl liquid around in a container
Change the beginning blend to a different blend.

_ _ _ _ _

An appliance used to cook outdoors.
Change the beginning blend to a different blend.

_ _ _ _ _
1

A fancy lace edge
Add a consonant.

_ _ _ _ _

A small stream or trickle
Change the vowel.

_ _ _ _

To flip over and over
Remove two consonants.

_ _ _ _

A rolled piece of paper
Change the beginning blend to a different blend.

_ _ _ _ _ _

A leisurely walk
Add a consonant.

_ _ _ _ _

A folklore creature (usually a giant or dwarf)
Change the beginning consonant to a blend.

_ _ _ _ _

A fee
Change the beginning consonant.

_ _ _ _

NAME: _____

Start at the bottom and climb your way up by
reading the clues to change the word in each step.

POLL

A large farm where cattle
and other animals are bred
Change the beginning blend to a single consonant.

_ _ _ _ _

To flinch or grow pale from shock
Change the final consonant to a digraph.

_ _ _ _ _

To have no taste
Change the beginning blend to a different blend.

_ _ _ _ _

Pituitary _____.
Remove a vowel and change one consonant.

_ _ _ _ _

To look quickly
Change the beginning blend to a different blend.

_ _ _ _ _
2

A country in Europe
Change the beginning blend to a different blend.

_ _ _ _ _
5

A way of standing or being placed
Change the final consonant to a vowel.

_ _ _ _ _
6

To stop or restrict
Remove the final consonant and add a digraph.

_ _ _ _ _

To balance on both feet
Remove one consonant.

_ _ _ _ _
3

NAME: _____

STRAND

Start at the bottom and climb your way up by
reading the clues to change the word in each step.

Radiating light
Add a consonant.

— — — — — —

The opposite of left
Remove one consonant.

— — — — —

Something that causes you to be scared
Change the beginning blend to a different blend.

— — — — —

The action of flying
Change the beginning blend to a different blend.

— — — — —

A difficult situation
Change the beginning blend to a different blend.

— — — — —

Small or trivial
Add a consonant.

— — — — —

The opposite of dark
Change the beginning consonant.

— — — —

The opposite of loose
Change the beginning consonant.

— — — — —
4

The opposite of day
Remove one consonant.

— — — — —
7

NAME: _____

KNIGHT

Start at the bottom and climb your way up by
reading the clues to change the word in each step.

A mechanism that holds jewelry together
Add a consonant.

_ _ _ _ _

To put your hands together repeatedly
Change the final consonant.

_ _ _ _

A crustacean that lives in the ocean.
Change the beginning blend to a different blend.

_ _ _ _

To shut forcefully
Change the vowel.

_ _ _ _

An impoverished living place
Change the beginning blend to a different blend.

_ _ _ _

A purple fruit
Remove one consonant.

_ _ _ _

Vertical measure
Change the beginning digraph to a blend.

_ _ _ _ _

A digit on your hand
Change the beginning blend to a digraph.

_ _ _ _ _

A small piece of bread
Change the beginning consonant to a blend.

_ _ _ _ _

NAME: _____

Start at the bottom and climb your way up by
reading the clues to change the word in each step.

DUMB

A piece of clothing worn in the colder months.
Change the final digraph to a single consonant.

→ _ _ _ _

A person who guides a team
Change one of the vowels.

→ _ _ _ _

A piece of furniture for more than one person to sit on.
Remove a consonant.

→ _ _ _ _

To fold your body into a small, low position
Change the beginning blend to a different blend.

→ _ _ _ _

A miserable person
Change the beginning blend to a different blend.

→ _ _ _ _

SLOUCH

NAME: _____

Start at the bottom and climb your way up by reading the clues to change the word in each step.

After you've completed the five prior word ladders, complete the riddle below by matching the numbered letters from the ladders to the corresponding numbers on the answer line.

RIDDLE #7

What goes away as soon as you talk about it?

_ _ _ _ _ _ _
3   4   1   5   7   2   6

The past tense of rise
Remove a consonant.

— — — —

A type of writing
Change the beginning digraph to a blend.

— — — —

The past tense of choose
Add a consonant.

— — — —

A hollow rubber tube for water to flow through
Remove one of the vowels.

— — — —

A place to live
Change the beginning consonant.

— — — —
1

The singular form of lice
Change the beginning consonant.

— — — —

A small rodent
Change one of the vowels.

— — — —

A large horned forest animal
Change the beginning consonant.

— — — —

The opposite of tight
Change the beginning consonant.

— — — —

NAME: _____

Start at the bottom and climb your way up by
reading the clues to change the word in each step.

GOOSE

WORD LADDER 37

To rip or tear away
Remove a vowel.

_ _ _ _ _

A vertical or horizontal line
Add two consonants.

_ _ _ _ _

Ready to pick or eat
Change a vowel.

_ _ _ _

Coiled string, jute or vine
Change a consonant.

_ _ _ _

To do something over and over again/repetition
Remove a consonant.

_ _ _ _ _

Past tense of write
Change a vowel.

_ _ _ _ _

To make markings on paper with a pen, pencil or other tool.
Add a consonant.

_ _ _ _ _

An important ceremony or act
Change the beginning consonant.

_ _ _ _

An area of ground where something is constructed.
Change the beginning consonant.

_ _ _ _

NAME: _____

Start at the bottom and climb your way up by reading the clues to change the word in each step.

BITE

To lift
Change the beginning consonant.

— — — — —

Slightly wet
Add a vowel.

— — — —

Opposite of least
Change the beginning consonant.

— — — —

A wooden structure sticking out of the ground.
Change the vowel.

— — — —

Opposite of future
Change the beginning consonant.

— — — —

The crew in a play or other acting show
Change the final consonant.

— — — —
2

A large container used for holding liquids
Change the beginning consonant.

— — — —
3

A job
Change the beginning consonant.

— — — —

A face covering to disguise
Add a consonant.

— — — —

NAME: _____

ASK

Start at the bottom and climb your way up by
reading the clues to change the word in each step.

A body part for chewing and talking
Change the beginning consonant.

$\_$ $\_$ $\_$ $\_$

The direction opposite of north
Change a consonant into a vowel and change another vowel.

$\_$ $\_$ $\_$ $\_$

A slow moving animal in the rainforest
Remove a vowel and the ending digraph and add a different digraph.

$\_$ $\_$ $\_$ $\_$

A swamp
Remove the beginning consonant and add a blend.

$\_$ $\_$ $\_$ $\_$

A main branch of a tree
Remove a consonant.

$\_$ $\_$ $\_$ $\_$

Past tense of buy
Remove a consonant.

$\_$ $\_$ $\_$ $\_$

Past tense of bring
Remove the beginning consonant and add a blend.

$\_$ $\_$ $\_$ $\_$

Past tense of fight
Change the beginning consonant.

$\_$ $\_$ $\_$ $\_$

To have looked for
Add a consonant.

$\_$ $\_$ $\_$ $\_$

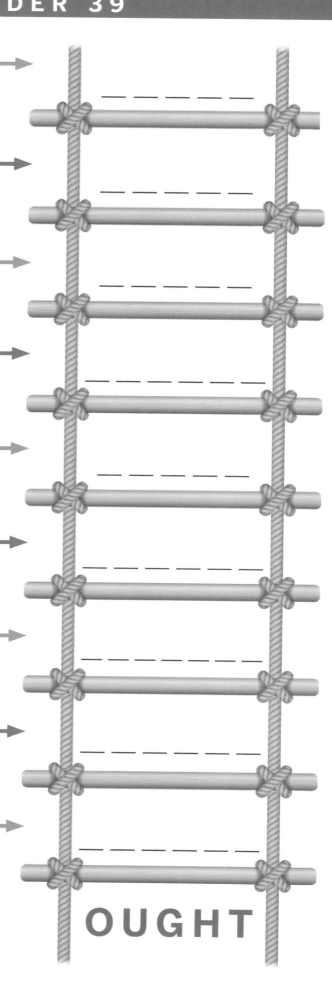

NAME: _____

Start at the bottom and climb your way up by reading the clues to change the word in each step.

OUGHT

To close your eyes a little to see more clearly
Remove the beginning 3-letter blend and replace it with a consonant digraph blend.

_ _ _ _ _ _

To run quickly for a short time
Change one letter in the 3-letter blend.

_ _ _ _ _ _

A long thin strip of wood, used to hold something immobile
Change the beginning blend to a 3-letter blend.

_ _ _ _ _ _

A short time
Add a consonant.

_ _ _ _ _

A value of color
Change the beginning consonant.

_ _ _ _

MINT

NAME: _____

Start at the bottom and climb your way up by reading the clues to change the word in each step.

After you've completed the five prior word ladders, complete the riddle below by matching the numbered letters from the ladders to the corresponding numbers on the answer line.

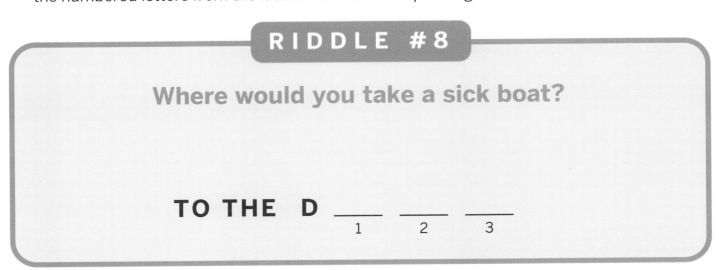

RIDDLE #8

Where would you take a sick boat?

TO THE D ___ ___ ___
              1   2   3

I had to ____ around in the dark looking for the light switch.
Change the vowel.

____ ____ ____ ____ ____
5

The ____ rolled on the floor before I could eat it.
Change a consonant.

____ ____ ____ ____
1

The dancer moved with ____ and certainty.
Change the beginning blend to a different blend.

____ ____ ____ ____ ____

The person vanished without a _____.
Remove a consonant.

____ ____ ____ ____

The musician put the audience into a _____.
Change the beginning blend to a different blend.

____ ____ ____ ____ ____

The horse will gallop and ____ across the arena.
Change the vowel.

____ ____ ____ ____ ____

The _____ will succeed the queen on the throne
Remove the beginning consonant and add a blend.

____ ____ ____ ____ ____

I _____ everytime I see someone get hurt.
Change the beginning consonant.

____ ____ ____ ____ ____

I have not been to the beach ____last summer.
Change the beginning consonant.

____ ____ ____ ____ ____

NAME: _____

Start at the bottom and climb your way up by reading the clues to change the word in each step.

MINCE

9

The alligator's snapping teeth will ____ its prey's flesh.
Remove a consonant.

— — — — —

Tik Tok is a new social media _____.
Change the beginning blend to a different blend.

— — — — —

I can't ____ a lot of money on my new bike.
Change the beginning blend to a different blend.

— — — —
2

The baker will ____ all of the ingredients together to make the cake.
Add a consonant.

— — — —

Will you ___ me a pencil?
Change the beginning consonant.

— — — —

I will ____ you a card in the mail.
Change the beginning consonant.

— — —

The rancher will ____ the fence where it is broken.
Change the beginning consonant.

— — — —
3

We will have to ____ for ourselves for dinner tonight.
Change the beginning consonant.

— — — —

The rubber band will ____ and twist.
Add a consonant.

— — — —

NAME: _____

END

Start at the bottom and climb your way up by reading the clues to change the word in each step.

The fox will _____ along quietly looking for its prey.
Change a consonant.

_ _ _ _ _

I had to ____ my eyes in the bright sunshine.
Change the vowel.

_ _ _ _

An artist loves to begin to draw on a _____ canvas.
Change a vowel and a consonant.

_ _ _ _

My friend lives one _____ away.
Change the beginning blend and vowel.

_ _ _ _
8

There was too much ____ in the rope and the horse got away.
Change the beginning digraph to a blend.

_ _ _ _

We set up a fishing _____ on the ice to protect us from the cold.
Change the vowel.

_ _ _ _

I love to ____ corn on the cob in the summer.
Change the beginning blend to a digraph.

_ _ _ _
4

Our truck got ____ in the mud.
Remove a consonant.

_ _ _ _ _
7

The lightning _____ the willow tree.
Add a consonant.

_ _ _ _ _
6

NAME: _____

Start at the bottom and climb your way up by reading the clues to change the word in each step.

TRUCK

WORD LADDER 44

My ankle began to ___ as soon as I twisted it.
Change the beginning blend to a different blend.

→ _ _ _ _ _

I can ____ many difficult words.
Change the vowel.

→ _ _ _ _ _

The oil ____ polluted the ocean water.
Change the beginning blend to a different blend.

→ _ _ _ _ _

Please sit ___ to have your picture taken.
Change the vowel.

→ _ _ _ _

We put the horse in the ____ near the barn door.
Change a consonant.

→ _ _ _ _

The corn ____ will grow as tall as 6 feet!
Change the beginning digraph to a blend.

→ _ _ _ _ _

The artist made the sidewalk art using only white ____.
Remove the beginning consonant and add a digraph.

→ _ _ _ _ _

The gardener will ____ at the idea of planting before May 31st.
Change the beginning consonant.

→ _ _ _ _

I ____ the dog every day before I go to school.
Change the beginning consonant.

→ _ _ _ _

NAME: _____

Start at the bottom and climb your way up by reading the clues to change the word in each step.

TALK

The ____ necklace looked lovely against her black dress.
Add a consonant.

_ _ _ _ _

The audience will ___ with laughter when the comedian begins his act.
Change the beginning consonant.

_ _ _ _

A ___ swam right up to my kayak in the ocean.
Change the beginning consonant.

_ _ _ _

I hope the cut on your hand will ____ soon.
Change one of the vowels.

_ _ _ _

Anne had blisters on her left ____ from her new shoes.
Remove a consonant.

_ _ _ _

WHEEL

NAME: _____

Start at the bottom and climb your way up by reading the clues to change the word in each step.

....

After you've completed the five prior word ladders, complete the riddle below by matching the numbered letters from the ladders to the corresponding numbers on the answer line.

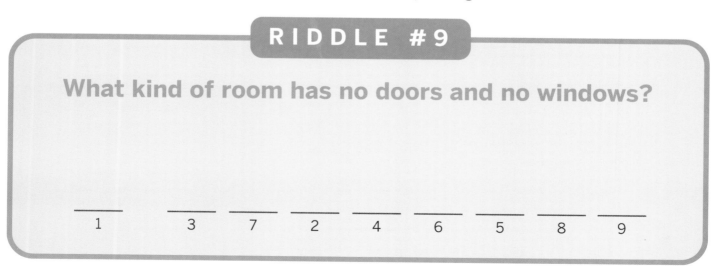

RIDDLE #9

What kind of room has no doors and no windows?

___   ___ ___ ___ ___ ___ ___ ___ ___
 1   3   7   2   4   6   5   8   9

The skateboarders built a _____ to ride on.
Change the beginning consonant.

_ _ _ _ _

A device that gives off light
Remove one consonant.

_ _ _

I put a _____ on the hose to stop the water.
Change the vowel.

_ _ _ _

A bunch (usually of something in nature)
Change the beginning blend to a different blend.

_ _ _ _ _
   2

Fat or chubby
Add a consonant.

_ _ _ _

A purple fruit
Change the beginning blend to a different blend.

_ _ _ _

To feel sad
Change the final vowel to a consonant.

_ _ _ _

I put _____ on the broken handle to fix it.
Change the beginning blend to a different blend.

_ _ _ _

My favorite color is _____.
Change the beginning consonant.

_ _ _ _
   1

NAME: _____

CLUE

Start at the bottom and climb your way up by reading the clues to change the word in each step.

WORD LADDER 47

The opposite of hot
Change a consonant.

⟶ _ _ _ _

A young male horse
Change the beginning consonant.

⟶ _ _ _ _

The measure of electrical force
Change the beginning consonant.

⟶ _ _ _ _
6

An otter lives in a ____.
Change the final consonant.

⟶ _ _ _ _

Please ____ my hand when we cross the street.
Change the beginning consonant.

⟶ _ _ _ _

____ and silver are popular metals for jewelry.
Change the beginning consonant.

⟶ _ _ _ _

We found ____ in the corner of the shower.
Change the vowel.

⟶ _ _ _ _

I like my chicken wings to be ____.
Change the beginning consonant.

⟶ _ _ _ _

The opposite of tame
Remove the beginning digraph and add a single consonant.

⟶ _ _ _ _

NAME: _____

Start at the bottom and climb your way up by reading the clues to change the word in each step.

CHILD

Being from Greece
Change the beginning blend to a different blend.

_ _ _ _ _
3

A stream or brook
Change the beginning consonant to a blend.

_ _ _ _ _

Seven days
Change the final consonant.

_ _ _ _

Cry
Remove one consonant.

_ _ _ _

Please ____ the dirt off the floor.
Change the beginning blend to a different blend.

_ _ _ _ _
7

We rode our bikes up a ____ hill.
Change the beginning blend to a different blend.

_ _ _ _ _

I like to ____ for 8 hours each night.
Change the final consonant.

_ _ _ _ _

A mix of snow and rain.
Change the beginning blend to a different blend.

_ _ _ _ _

The opposite of sour
Change one vowel.

_ _ _ _ _

NAME: _____

Start at the bottom and climb your way up by
reading the clues to change the word in each step.

SWEAT

Baseball is my favorite ____.
Add a consonant.

— — — — —

The captain docked the ship in the _____.
Change the vowel.

— — — —

A piece of a larger item
Change the beginning consonant.

— — — —

A pastry with a fruit filling
Remove a consonant.

— — — —

The opposite of end
Change the beginning blend to a different blend.

— — — —

I read a lot so that I can be _____.
Remove the beginning digraph and add a blend.

— — — —
5

The graph was written on a large paper ____.
Remove one vowel and change a consonant.

— — — —

To run quickly toward something.
Change the beginning consonant to a digraph.

— — — —

A flat-bottomed boat
Change the beginning consonant.

— — — —
9

NAME: _____

Start at the bottom and climb your way up by
reading the clues to change the word in each step.

LARGE

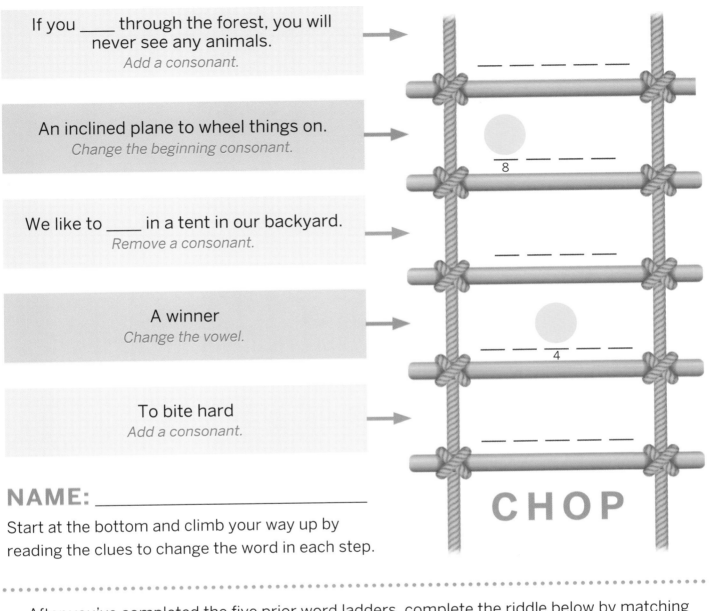

If you ____ through the forest, you will never see any animals.
Add a consonant.

An inclined plane to wheel things on.
Change the beginning consonant.

We like to ____ in a tent in our backyard.
Remove a consonant.

A winner
Change the vowel.

To bite hard
Add a consonant.

CHOP

NAME: _____

Start at the bottom and climb your way up by reading the clues to change the word in each step.

After you've completed the five prior word ladders, complete the riddle below by matching the numbered letters from the ladders to the corresponding numbers on the answer line.

RIDDLE #10

What fruit can never cheer up?

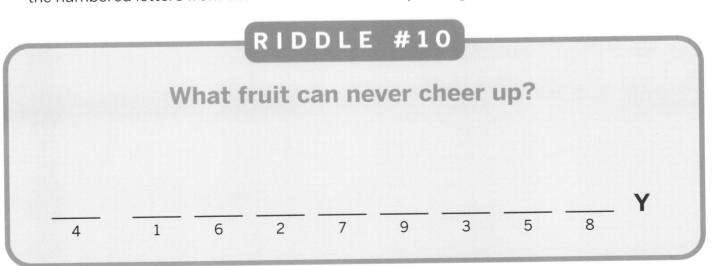

____ ____ ____ ____ ____ ____ ____ ____ ____ **Y**
4   1   6   2   7   9   3   5   8

Partially burn
Remove a consonant.

→ _ _ _ _ _

The ____ will show the results of the survey.
Change the beginning consonant to a digraph.

→ _ _ _ _ _
      1

To move quickly
Change the vowel.

→ _ _ _ _

Please remove the ____ from your boots before coming into the house.
Change the beginning blend to a single consonant.

→ _ _ _ _

Behave as though attracted to someone.
Remove three letters and add a blend.

→ _ _ _ _

The juice will ____ out of the box if you squeeze it.
Remove one consonant and replace with a digraph.

→ _ _ _ _

She wore a ____ and blouse to dinner.
Change the beginning digraph to a blend.

→ _ _ _ _

A piece of clothing worn on the top of your body
Change the vowel.

→ _ _ _ _ _
      2

Opposite of tall
Change one consonant.

→ _ _ _ _ _

NAME: _____

Start at the bottom and climb your way up by reading the clues to change the word in each step.

SNORT

To stir or mix, as butter
Change the beginning consonant to a digraph.

_ _ _ _ _

The forest fire will ____ for days.
Change the vowel.

_ _ _ _

The farm animals all have stalls in the _____.
Change the beginning consonant.

_ _ _ _

A textile that is used to knit.
Change the final consonant.

_ _ _ _

Outdoor grassy area usually surrounding a house
Change the beginning consonant.

_ _ _ _

Fat or grease for cooking
Change the beginning consonant.

_ _ _ _

His favorite ____ was the ace of spades.
Change the beginning consonant.

_ _ _ _

A poet
Change the beginning consonant.

_ _ _ _

The opposite of easy
Remove one consonant.

_ _ _ _

NAME: _____

Start at the bottom and climb your way up by reading the clues to change the word in each step.

SHARD

The opposite of finish
Change the final vowel.

‾ ‾ ‾ ‾

It is not good to _____ at the sun.
Add a vowel.

_ _ _ _
3

A point of light in the night sky
Remove one consonant.

_ _ _ _ _

Bare in appearance
Change the beginning blend to a different blend.

_ _ _ _

I put a new _____ plug in the motorcycle to make it run better.
Change the beginning digraph to a blend.

_ _ _ _

My favorite _____ is the Great White.
Change the beginning consonant to a digraph.

_ _ _ _
7

The opposite of light
Change the beginning consonant.

_ _ _ _

The baseball left a round ___ on my arm when it hit me.
Change the beginning consonant.

_ _ _ _

What a dog does
Change the beginning consonant.

_ _ _ _

NAME: _____

Start at the bottom and climb your way up by reading the clues to change the word in each step.

PARK

To cut with a harsh sweeping motion
Change the beginning blend to a different blend.

— — — — —

To conflict with
Add a consonant.

— — — —

I gave the shop owner all the _____ I had for my new bike.
Change the beginning consonant.

— — — —
4

I like to ____ my potatoes and carrots together.
Change the final blend to a digraph.

— — — —
5

The ____ of the ship was taller than a two-story building.
Change the vowel.

— — — —

The opposite of least
Change the beginning consonant.

— — — —

I had to bring a letter to the _____ office.
Change the final vowel to a consonant.

— — — —
6

To hold your body still in a special position for a certain amount of time
Remove a vowel.

— — — —

The dancer had to recover her _____ after she stumbled.
Change the beginning consonant.

— — — — —

NAME: _____

NOISE

Start at the bottom and climb your way up by reading the clues to change the word in each step.

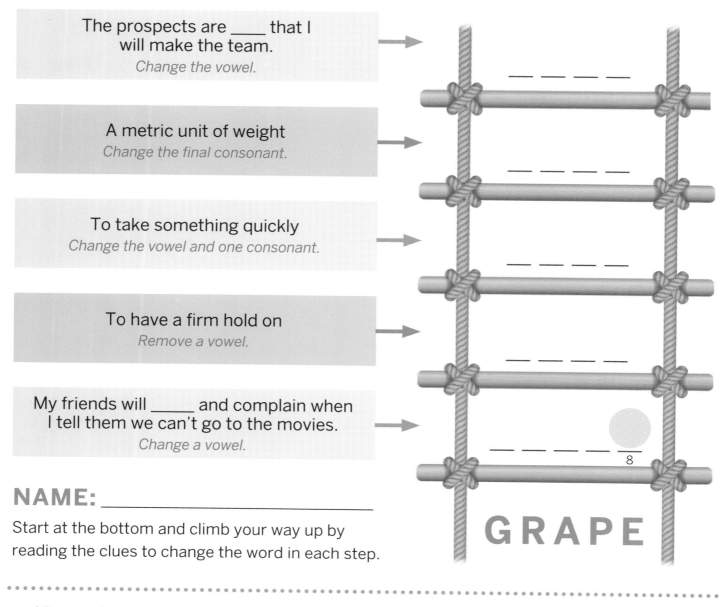

The prospects are _____ that I will make the team.
Change the vowel.

_ _ _ _ _

A metric unit of weight
Change the final consonant.

_ _ _ _ _

To take something quickly
Change the vowel and one consonant.

_ _ _ _ _

To have a firm hold on
Remove a vowel.

_ _ _ _

My friends will _____ and complain when I tell them we can't go to the movies.
Change a vowel.

_ _ _ _ _
          8

NAME: _____

Start at the bottom and climb your way up by reading the clues to change the word in each step.

GRAPE

After you've completed the five prior word ladders, complete the riddle below by matching the numbered letters from the ladders to the corresponding numbers on the answer line.

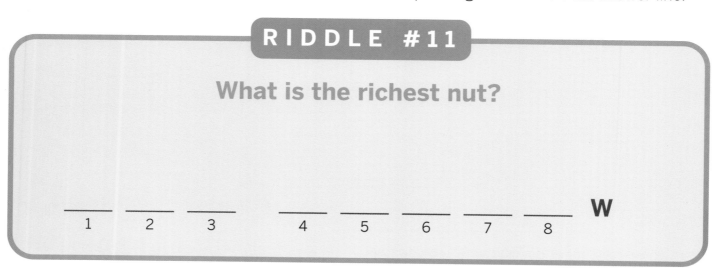

RIDDLE #11

What is the richest nut?

___ ___ ___   ___ ___ ___ ___ ___ **W**
 1   2   3   4   5   6   7   8

Art class is my favorite subject because I like to _____.
Remove a consonant.

— — — — —

The past tense of draw.
Change a consonant.

— — — — —

Would you rather have ____ or brains?
Change the vowel.

— — — — —
4

____ is a mixture of all colors together.
Add a consonant.

— — — — —

The man furrowed his ____ when he was confused.
Change the vowel.

— — — —

My mom drinks a strong ____ of coffee every morning.
Change the beginning digraph to a blend.

— — — —
1

To grind food in your mouth
Change the beginning consonant to a digraph.

— — — —

A wooden seat in church
Change the beginning consonant.

— — — —

Morning moisture on plants
Change the beginning consonant.

— — —

NAME: _____

FEW

Start at the bottom and climb your way up by reading the clues to change the word in each step.

A stringed instrument you play with a bow
Change the beginning consonant.

Beginning, _____, end
Change a vowel.

To make a mess of things
Change the beginning consonant.

The football team got in a ____ to determine their next play.
Change the beginning consonant.

To snuggle together
Change the beginning consonant.

The toddler jumped in the rain ____.
Change one vowel into a different vowel, and one vowel into a consonant.

2

A type of dog
Change the beginning consonant.

To draw loosely and with no plan
Change the beginning consonant.

Pasta
Change the first two vowels.

NAME: _____

Start at the bottom and climb your way up by reading the clues to change the word in each step.

NEEDLE

Those scissors are very _____.
Change the final vowel to a consonant.

— — — — —

I will _____ my snack with you.
Remove the beginning consonant and add a digraph.

— — — — —
5

The opposite of neglect
Change a vowel.

— — — —

The middle of an apple
Remove a consonant.

— — — —

Points in a game
Change the beginning blend to a different blend.

— — — —

I had to go to the shoe _____ to
get new sneakers.
Change the beginning blend to a different blend.

— — — —

To have spoken bad words
Add a consonant.

— — — — —

The past tense of wear
Change the beginning consonant.

— — — —

Microscopic opening in your skin
Change the beginning consonant.

— — — —

NAME: _____

Start at the bottom and climb your way up by
reading the clues to change the word in each step.

MORE

A joke that plays on words
Change a vowel and the double consonants.

———————

The baby will shake her _____ and laugh.
Change the beginning consonant.

———————

The rancher moved the _____ to another field.
Change the beginning consonant.

———————

A fight
Change the beginning consonant.

———————

To tell on someone
Change the beginning consonant and one other consonant.

———————

Loose, sleeveless garment; cloak
Change a consonant.

———————

To twist and bend together in a disorderly way
Change a vowel.

— — — — —
3

The senator will _____ with the crowd.
Change the beginning consonant.

———————

I heard the coins _____ in his pants pocket.
Change the beginning consonant.

———————

NAME: _____

Start at the bottom and climb your way up by reading the clues to change the word in each step.

TINGLE

WORD LADDER 60

_____, _____ little star
Change the beginning 3-letter blend to a 2-letter blend.

→ _ _ _ _

I will ____ the corn with salt.
Change the beginning blend to a 3-letter blend.

→ _ _ _ _

If my clothes have a _____, I will iron them.
Change the beginning blend to a different blend.

→ _ _ _ _

Small creases or wrinkles
Change one vowel and one consonant.

→ _ _ _ _

The sound a fire makes
Change the beginning digraph to a blend.

→ _ _ _ _

NAME: _____

Start at the bottom and climb your way up by
reading the clues to change the word in each step.

SHACKLE

··

After you've completed the five prior word ladders, complete the riddle below by matching
the numbered letters from the ladders to the corresponding numbers on the answer line.

RIDDLE #12

What has a head, a tail, is brown, and has no legs?

____ ____ ____ ____ ____ **Y**
 5   2   1   3   4

ANSWER KEY

Ladder #1: flute, lute, cute, jute, mute, mate, rate, crate, grate, grape

Ladder #2: close, chose, those, hose, nose, pose, rose, rise, wise, guise

Ladder #3: shade, spade, trade, grade, glade, blade, wade, wide, wire, wore

Ladder #4: cure, pure, lure, sure, sore, sort, port, sport, snort, short

Ladder #5: month, moth, math, match, patch, pitch

Riddle #1: a clock

Ladder #6: like, lake, flake, shake, snake, stake, stoke, spoke, spike, pike

Ladder #7: fame, frame, blame, flame, lame, lime, time, tome, tame, game

Ladder #8: brave, crave, grave, grove, cove, rote, rose, prose, close, chose

Ladder #9: mice, dice, lice, slice, slick, stick, stock, tock, lock, clock

Ladder #10: early, earl, ear, tear, pear, pearl

Riddle #2: your name

Ladder #11: plan, plane, lane, vane, vine, pine, wine, whine, shine, shrine

Ladder #12: hide, wide, tide, side, bride, chide, glide, slide, snide, stride

Ladder #13: caw, claw, flaw, law, lawn, yawn, drawn, draw, gnaw, thaw

Ladder #14: beach, breach, bleach, leach, teach, peach, preach, reach, read, reap

Ladder #15: frost, lost, cost, cast, cash, clash

Riddle #3: a promise

Ladder #16: sweep, steep, sleep, sheep, seep, weep, keep, deep, deer, steer

Ladder #17: rain, train, strain, stain, slain, plain, trait, strait, gait, bait

Ladder #18: toad, road, goad, goal, coal, coat, goat, gloat, float, moat

Ladder #19: trout, stout, sprout, spout, snout, shout, scout, scour, sour, hour

Ladder #20: loon, moon, soon, soot, boot, boat

Riddle #4: a stamp

Ladder #21: good, wood, hood, hook, shook, brook, broom, bloom, loom, room

Ladder #22: soil, foil, toil, boil, broil, spoil, coil, coin, join, groin

Ladder #23: spread, dead, head, lead, read, bread, dread, tread, thread, threat

Ladder #24: pound, bound, ground, grout, trout, stout, spout, sprout, rout, round

Ladder #25: horn, thorn, torn, born, burn, burp

Riddle #5: popcorn

Ladder #26: hung, lung, clung, flung, flunk, spunk, trunk, stunk, stink, slink

Ladder #27: fowl, howl, growl, scowl, prowl, prow, crow, crew, drew, grew

Ladder #28: watch, hatch, match, latch, patch, pitch, ditch, witch, switch, stitch

Ladder #29: badge, budge, fudge, judge, nudge, drudge, grudge, sludge, smudge, trudge

Ladder #30: prone, prune, June, tune, tone, stone

Riddle #6: light